Early American Wisdom

Early American Wisdom

A Treasury of Quotations

Arranged by Jackie Corley

hatherleigh
Improve your life. Change your world.

Hatherleigh Press is committed to preserving
and protecting the natural resources of the earth.
Environmentally responsible and sustainable practices are
embraced within the company's mission statement.

Visit us at www.hatherleighpress.com and register online
for free offers, discounts, special events, and more.

Early American Wisdom

Library of Congress Cataloging-in-Publication Data is available.
ISBN: 978-1-57826-893-1

Printed in the United States
10 9 8 7 6 5 4 3 2 1

"Once you learn to read you will be forever free."

—FREDERICK DOUGLASS

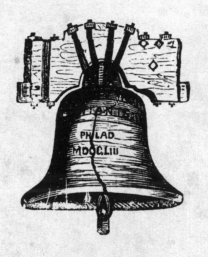

Contents

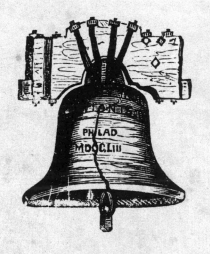

Introduction

AT A TIME WHEN THE PRESENT AND THE future both seem equally tumultuous and uncertain, it is our history which anchors us in our shared past. Our founding fathers and mothers encountered profound challenges in realizing a vision for America. There were no guarantees of life, liberty, or the pursuit of happiness, yet they relentlessly pursued their dream of building a new nation. Emboldened by the challenges they faced and resolute in creating opportunities for future generations, early Americans leaders, writers and philosophers shaped the language we use and the ideals we pursue to this day.

Early American Wisdom collects the aphorisms of Benjamin Franklin, the measured guidance of George Washington, the astute observations of Abigail Adams, Thomas Jefferson's musings on a temperate and virtuous life, and so much more.

The advice left behind by our Colonial and Revolutionary Era forebearers is uncanny in its continued relevance to our fast-paced, technology-driven age. They urged patience, the mining of past mistakes to gain wisdom. They encouraged productivity as a path toward happiness. Above all, they balanced optimism with a clear-eyed vision of both the foibles and potential for humanity.

Early
American
Wisdom

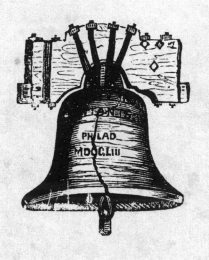

Patience, Patience

Staying decisive and moving fast are equally prized in our technology-driven era. Yet early American leaders and writers speak to the power of deliberate, measured thoughts and actions. Moving slowly and judiciously through life allows us to avoid errors in judgment.

He that can have patience can have what he will.

—BENJAMIN FRANKLIN

Be not deceived with the first appearances of things, but give thyself time to be in the right.

—WILLIAM PENN

When angry count to ten before you speak. If very angry, count to one hundred.

—THOMAS JEFFERSON

Suspicion is far more apt to be wrong than right; oftener unjust than just. It is no friend to virtue, and always an enemy to happiness.

—HOSEA BALLOU

Truth is powerful and it prevails.

—SOJOURNER TRUTH

There is no great achievement that is not the result of patient working and waiting.

—JOSIAH GILBERT HOLLAND

Never do today what you can put off till tomorrow. Delay may give clearer light as to what is best to be done.

—AARON BURR

If thou thinkest twice, before thou speakest once, thou wilt speak twice the better for it.

—WILLIAM PENN

Brevity and conciseness are the parents of correction.

—HOSEA BALLOU

Fire hath its force abated by water, not by wind; and anger must by allayed by cold words, and not by blustering threats.

—ANNE BRADSTREET

How much pain have cost us the evils which have never happened.

—THOMAS JEFFERSON

A work of real merit finds favor at last.

—AMOS BRONSON ALCOTT

Calmness is the cradle of power.

—JOSIAH GILBERT HOLLAND

I always considered an idle Life, as a real evil, but, a life of such hurry, such constant hurry, leaves us scarcely a moment for reflection or for the discharge of any other then the most immediate and pressing concerns.

—EDWARD RUTLEDGE

Always take hold of things by the smooth handle.

—THOMAS JEFFERSON

When in doubt, don't.

—BENJAMIN FRANKLIN

While despair is preying on the mind, time and its effects are preying on despair; and certain it is, the dismal vision will face away, and Forgetfulness, with her sister Ease, will change the scene.

—THOMAS PAINE

When the sword is once drawn, the passions of men observe no bounds of moderation.

—ALEXANDER HAMILTON

It is always better to have no ideas than false ones; to believe nothing, than to believe what is wrong.

—THOMAS JEFFERSON

Distrust naturally creates distrust, and by nothing is good-will and kind conduct more speedily changed than by invidious jealousies and uncandid imputations, whether expressed or implied.

—JOHN JAY

Be always sure you're right—then go ahead.

—DAVID CROCKETT

Hard words are very rarely useful. Real firmness
is good for everything. Strut is good for nothing.

—ALEXANDER HAMILTON

We may give advice, but we cannot give conduct.

—BENJAMIN FRANKLIN

We cannot act with too much caution in our
disputes. Anger produces anger; and differences
that might be accommodated by kind and
respectful behaviour, may by imprudence be
changed to an incurable rage.

—JOHN DICKINSON

There is no royal road to anything, one thing at a time, all things in succession. That which grows fast, withers as rapidly. That which grows slowly, endures.

—JOSIAH GILBERT HOLLAND

Make haste slowly.

—BENJAMIN FRANKLIN

Delay is preferable to error.

—THOMAS JEFFERSON

Believe nothing against another, but upon good authority: nor report what may hurt another, unless it be a greater hurt to others to conceal it.

—WILLIAM PENN

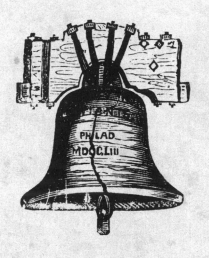

Working for
Your Wisdom

Intelligence is an innate characteristic; wisdom can only be arrived at through life experience. Early Americans valued wisdom as knowledge earned and therefore prized above native intelligence. Wisdom provides guideposts for life through lessons learned from past mistakes.

Knowledge will forever govern ignorance, and a people who mean to be their own governors, must arm themselves with the power knowledge gives.

—JAMES MADISON

I have but one lamp by which my feet are guided, and that is the lamp of experience. I know of no way of judging of the future but by the past.

—PATRICK HENRY

They that will not be counselled cannot be helped.

—BENJAMIN FRANKLIN

Authority without wisdom is like a heavy ax without an edge—fitter to bruise than polish.

—ANNE BRADSTREET

Men give me credit for some genius. All the genius I have lies in this; when I have a subject in hand, I study it profoundly. Day and night it is before me. My mind becomes pervaded with it. Then the effort that I have made is what people are pleased to call the fruit of genius. It is the fruit of labor and thought.

—ALEXANDER HAMILTON

Error often is to be preferred to indecision.

—AARON BURR

Ignorance is the womb of monsters.

—HENRY WARD BEECHER

Learning is not attained by chance, it must be sought for with ardor and attended to with diligence.

—ABIGAIL ADAMS

To be ignorant of one's ignorance is the malady of the ignorant.

—AMOS BRONSON ALCOTT

Experience is the oracle of truth; and where its responses are unequivocal, they ought to be conclusive and sacred.

—JAMES MADISON

Sorrow makes men sincere, and anguish makes them earnest.

—HENRY WARD BEECHER

Experience keeps a dear school, but fools will learn in no other.

—BENJAMIN FRANKLIN

I know of no way of judging the future but by the past.

—PATRICK HENRY

A morsel of genuine history is so rare a thing as to be always valuable.

—THOMAS JEFFERSON

Observation more than books and experience more than persons, are the prime educators.

—AMOS BRONSON ALCOTT

Genius is not a single power, but a combination of great powers. It reasons, but it is not reasoning; it judges, but it is not judgment; imagines, but it is not imagination; it feels deeply and fiercely, but it is not passion. It is neither, because it is all.

—EDWIN PERCY WHIPPLE

Freedom can exist only in the society of knowledge. Without learning, men are incapable of knowing their right and where learning is confined to few people, liberty can be neither equal nor universal.

—BENJAMIN RUSH

The world is a severe schoolmaster, for its frowns are less dangerous than its smiles and flatteries, and it is a difficult task to keep in the path of wisdom.

—PHILLIS WHEATLEY

Philosophy is common sense with big words.

—JAMES MADISON

Wisdom with an inheritance is good, but wisdom without an inheritance is better than an inheritance without wisdom.

—ANNE BRADSTREET

Some people can be reasoned into sense, and others must be shocked into it.

—THOMAS PAINE

I take it to be from the greatest extremes, both in virtue and in vice, that the uniformly virtuous and reformed in life can derive the greatest and most salutary truths and impressions.

—DEBORAH SAMPSON

One must spend time in gathering knowledge to give it out richly.

—EDMUND CLARENCE STEDMAN

If we mean to have heroes, statesmen and philosophers, we should have learned women.

—ABIGAIL ADAMS

Temperate, sincere, and intelligent inquiry and discussion are only to be dreaded by the advocates of error.

—BENJAMIN RUSH

Experience is a severe preceptor, but it teaches useful truths, and however harsh, is always honest. Be calm and dispassionate, and listen to what it tells us.

—JOHN JAY

Advice is not a gift, but a debt that the old owe to the young.

—JAMES FENIMORE COOPER

It is the mind that makes the body.

—SOJOURNER TRUTH

Receive good counsel of the wise, not let
Unshallow'd lips provoke, or cause to fret.
Be wise and virt'ous, modest, chaste and grave,
Increase in learning, practice what you have,
Enter the list 'gainst sin, with courage brave.

—MARTHA WADSWORTH
BREWSTER

Ignorance and superstition ever bear a close and mathematical relation to each other.

—JAMES FENIMORE COOPER

A little neglect may breed mischief: for want of a nail the shoe was lost; for want of a shoe the horse was lost; and for want of a horse the rider was lost.

—BENJAMIN FRANKLIN

To argue with a person who has renounced the use of reason is like administering medicine to the dead.

—THOMAS PAINE

Embracing
Challenge

Early Americans understood that change and the advance of civilization doesn't arrive passively. Hard work and sacrifice are required to enact lasting change.

All great and honorable actions are accompanied with great difficulties, and both must be enterprised and overcome with answerable courage.

—WILLIAM BRADFORD

The waves have rolled upon me, the billows are repeatedly broken over me, yet I am not sunk down.

—MERCY OTIS WARREN

Great difficulties may be surmounted by patience and perseverance.

—ABIGAIL ADAMS

Those who expect to reap the blessings of freedom must, like men, undergo the fatigue of supporting it.

—THOMAS PAINE

Perseverance and spirit have done wonders in all ages.

—GEORGE WASHINGTON

No great advance has ever been made in science, politics, or religion, without controversy.

—LYMAN BEECHER

Always do what you are afraid to do.

—MARY MOODY EMERSON

Be courteous to all, but intimate with few, and let those few be well tried before you give them your confidence. True friendship is a plant of slow growth, and must undergo and withstand the shocks of adversity before it is entitled to appellation.

—GEORGE WASHINGTON

We must make the best of those ills which cannot be avoided.

—ALEXANDER HAMILTON

God gives every bird its food, but He does not throw it into its nest.

—JOSIAH GILBERT HOLLAND

What we obtain too cheap, we esteem too lightly; it is dearness only that gives everything its value.

—THOMAS PAINE

Success is sweet and sweeter if long delayed and gotten through many struggles and defeats.

—AMOS BRONSON ALCOTT

Charity has its life in disasters, not in ventures.

—ROBERT CUSHMAN

If we had not winter, the spring would not be so pleasant; if we did not sometimes taste of adversity, prosperity would not be so welcome.

—ANNE BRADSTREET

Ninety-nine percent of failures come from people who make excuses.

—GEORGE WASHINGTON

Every problem is an opportunity in disguise.

—JOHN ADAMS

We climb to heaven most often on the ruins of our cherished plans, finding our failures were successes.

—AMOS BRONSON ALCOTT

We have too many high-sounding words, and too few actions that correspond with them.

—ABIGAIL ADAMS

Never abandon your vision. Keep reaching to further your dreams.

—BENJAMIN BANNEKER

Give me liberty or give me death!

—PATRICK HENRY

As I understand it, laws, commands, rules and edicts are for those who have not the light which makes plain the pathway.

—ANNE HUTCHINSON

No pain, no palm; no thornes, no throne; no gall, no glory; no cross, no crown.

—WILLIAM PENN

Those who trade liberty for security have neither.

—JOHN ADAMS

Great minds have purposes; others have wishes.

—WASHINGTON IRVING

Presumption should never make us neglect that which appears easy to us, nor despair make us lose courage at the sight of difficulties.

—BENJAMIN BANNEKER

The turning points of lives are not the great moments. The real crises are often concealed in occurrences so trivial in appearance that they pass unobserved.

—GEORGE WASHINGTON

Without a struggle, there can be no progress.

—FREDERICK DOUGLASS

If there must be trouble, let it be in my day, that my child may have peace.

—THOMAS PAINE

Great advantages are often attended with great inconveniences, and great minds called to severe trials.

—MERCY OTIS WARREN

A barking dog is often more useful than a sleeping lion.

—WASHINGTON IRVING

I must study politics and war, that our sons may have liberty to study mathematics and philosophy. Our sons ought to study mathematics and philosophy, geography, natural history and naval architecture, navigation, commerce and agriculture in order to give their children a right to study painting, poetry, music, architecture, statuary, tapestry and porcelain.

—JOHN ADAMS

These are times in which a genius would wish to live. It is not in the still calm of life, or in the repose of a pacific station, that great characters are formed. The habits of a vigorous mind are formed in contending with difficulties. Great necessities call out great virtues.

—ABIGAIL ADAMS

A Life of Good Character

Public accolades and celebration are worth little if your life isn't led by an inner compass directing you toward doing what's right. Early American writers and leaders championed good character and moral fortitude as hallmarks of a life well-lived.

Don't talk about what you have done or what you are going to do.

—THOMAS JEFFERSON

Character is a thing that will take care of itself; and all character that does not take care of itself is either very weak or utterly fictitious.

—JOSIAH GILBERT HOLLAND

If conscience disapproves, the loudest applauses of the world are of little value.

—JOHN ADAMS

Character is a fact, and that is much in a world
of pretense and concession.

—AMOS BRONSON ALCOTT

All greatness of character is dependent on
individuality.

—JAMES FENIMORE COOPER

Sublimity of character must come from sublimity
of motive.

—MARY MOODY EMERSON

Large streams from little fountains flow. Tall oaks from little acorns grow.

—DAVID EVERETT

To be good, and to do good, is all we have to do.

—JOHN ADAMS

Character gives splendor to youth and awe to wrinkled skin and gray hairs.

—RALPH WALDO EMERSON

Character is the governing element in life, and is above genius.

—FREDERICK SAUNDERS

Associate with men of good quality, if you esteem your own reputation; for it is better to be alone than in bad company.

—GEORGE WASHINGTON

It takes many good deeds to build a good reputation, and only one bad one to lose it.

—BENJAMIN FRANKLIN

There are two rules whereby we are to walk, one towards another: justice and mercy.

—JOHN WINTHROP

Liberty will not long survive the total extinction of morals.

—SAMUEL ADAMS

Character is impulse that has been reined down into steady continuances.

—CHARLES HENRY PARKHURST

Labor to keep alive in your breast that little spark of celestial fire, called Conscience.

—GEORGE WASHINGTON

Honesty, sincerity, and openness I esteem essential marks of a good mind.

—JOHN ADAMS

It is better for a man to die at peace with himself than to live haunted by an evil conscience!

—JAMES FENIMORE COOPER

Honor is not a virtue in itself, it is the mail behind which the virtues fight more securely.

—GEORGE H. CALVERT

Let your conversation be without malice or envy, for 'tis a sign of a tractable and commendable nature.

—GEORGE WASHINGTON

He is rich or poor according to what he is, not according to what he has.

—HENRY WARD BEECHER

Sin and shame ever go together; he that would be freed from the last must be sure to shun the company of the first.

—ANNE BRADSTREET

Virtue alone is sufficient to make a man great, glorious, and happy.

—BENJAMIN FRANKLIN

True liberty is not liberty to do evil as well as good.

—JOHN WINTHROP

Character cannot be constructed. It cannot be put together. It needs first of all a principle that is animated, and one, therefore, that is animating. It wants an impulse more glowing, determined, and passionate than anything we are possessed of naturally.

—CHARLES HENRY PARKHURST

The soul, like the body, lives by what it feeds on.

—JOSIAH GILBERT HOLLAND

There was never yet a truly great man that was not at the same time truly virtuous.

—BENJAMIN FRANKLIN

Whenever you do a thing, act as if all the world were watching.

—THOMAS JEFFERSON

A promise must never be broken.

—ALEXANDER HAMILTON

Be not apt to relate news, if you know not the truth thereof. Speak no evil of the absent, for it is unjust. Undertake not what you cannot perform, but be careful to keep your promise. There is but one straight course, and that is to seek truth, and pursue it steadily. Nothing but harmony, honesty, industry and frugality are necessary to make us a great and happy nation.

—GEORGE WASHINGTON

Ambition without principle never was long under the guidance of good sense.

—ALEXANDER HAMILTON

Conduct is more convincing than language.

—JOHN WOOLMAN

It is the indispensable duty of those, who maintain for themselves the rights of human nature, and who possess the obligations of Christianity, to extend their power and influence to the relief of every part of the human race from whatever burden or oppression they may unjustly labor under.

—BENJAMIN BANNEKER

Happiness is not the end of life: character is.

—HENRY WARD BEECHER

It is the duty of every man, as far as his ability extends, to detect and expose delusion and error.

—THOMAS PAINE

No man is wiser for his learning. It may administer matter to work in, or objects to work upon; but wit and wisdom are born with a man.

—JOHN SELDEN

It is better to offer no excuse than a bad one.

—GEORGE WASHINGTON

Let our lives be in accordance with our convictions of right, each striving to carry out our principles.

—LUCRETIA MOTT

To be good, and to do good, is the whole duty of man comprised in a few words.

—ABIGAIL ADAMS

Early enrush thy heart with moral virtues,
Whereby to rectify inverted nature:
Survey the globe of man, then turn thine eyes
To search through nature's obscure mysteries;
Envy may hiss in vain, at virt'ous minds,
Regent in her own breast, she sits enshrin'd.

—MARTHA WADSWORTH
BREWSTER

The life of a nation is secure only while the
nation is honest, truthful, and virtuous.

—FREDERICK DOUGLASS

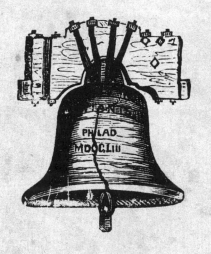

The Virtue
of Happiness,
The Happiness
of Virtue

Seeking out happiness isn't selfishness: indeed, it makes us better to our fellow human beings. Productivity complements the pursuit of happiness by giving us a foundation and structure for a life lived to the fullest.

Dost thou love life? Then do not squander time, for that is the stuff life is made of.

—BENJAMIN FRANKLIN

Every nation ought to have a right to provide for its own happiness.

—ALEXANDER HAMILTON

Preceptive wisdom that has not been vivified by life has in itself no affinity for life.

—JOSIAH GILBERT HOLLAND

Good humor is one of the preservatives of our peace and tranquility.

—THOMAS JEFFERSON

It is one of my sources of happiness never to desire a knowledge of other people's business.

—DOLLEY MADISON

Happiness depends more upon the internal frame of a person's own mind, than on the externals in the world.

—GEORGE WASHINGTON

I am determined to be cheerful and happy in whatever situation I may be. For I have also learned from experience that the greater part of our happiness, or misery depends on our dispositions and not on our circumstances. We carry the seeds of the one or the other about with us in our minds wherever we go.

—MARTHA WASHINGTON

The heart is wiser than the intellect.

—JOSIAH GILBERT HOLLAND

The less routine, the more life.

—AMOS BRONSON ALCOTT

The rule of my life is to make business a pleasure, and pleasure my business.

—AARON BURR

Determine never to be idle. No person will have occasion to complain of the want of time who never loses any. It is wonderful how much may be done if we are always doing.

—THOMAS JEFFERSON

There is a pleasure in the pathless woods,
There is a rapture on the lonely shore.

—JAMES FENIMORE COOPER

The person who does not know how to live while they are making a living is a poorer person after their wealth is won than when they started.

—JOSIAH GILBERT HOLLAND

Keep your business affairs in your own hands. It's the only way to be happy.

—MARTHA WASHINGTON

The sublimity connected with vastness, is familiar to every eye.

—JAMES FENIMORE COOPER

Beauty has no relation to price, rarity, or age.

—JOHN COTTON

Our ideals are our better selves.

—AMOS BRONSON ALCOTT

Diligence is the mother of good luck.

—BENJAMIN FRANKLIN

Idleness is paralysis.

—ROSWELL D. HITCHCOCK

The reward of a thing well done, is to have done it.

—RALPH WALDO EMERSON

Nor is a duty beneficial because it is commanded, but it is commanded because it is beneficial.

—BENJAMIN FRANKLIN

The temple of art is built in words.

—JOSIAH GILBERT HOLLAND

One of the greatest and simplest tools for learning more and growing is doing more.

—WASHINGTON IRVING

I begin to think, that a calm is not desirable in any situation in life. [...] Man was made for action and for bustle too, I believe.

—ABIGAIL ADAMS

No one has a greater asset for his business than a man's pride in his work.

—HOSEA BALLOU

There never was a good war or a bad peace.

—BENJAMIN FRANKLIN

If thou wouldst be happy and easy in thy family, above all things observe discipline.

—WILLIAM PENN

Mirth, and even cheerfulness, when employed as remedies in low spirits, are like hot water to a frozen limb.

—BENJAMIN RUSH

It is wonderful how much may be done if we are always doing.

—THOMAS JEFFERSON

Idleness is the sepulchre of a living man.

—JOSIAH GILBERT HOLLAND

Sweet words are like honey, a little may refresh, but too much gluts the stomach.

—ANNE BRADSTREET

Let us, then, be up and doing,
With a heart for any fate;
Still achieving, still pursuing,
Learn to labor and to wait.

—HENRY WADSWORTH
LONGFELLOW

The balm of life, a kind and faithful friend.

—MERCY OTIS WARREN

Pray that no sleep may seize upon your eyes, nor slumber upon your eyelids until your thoughts have seriously, calmly, and unchangeably fixed.

—ROGER WILLIAMS

I am only fond of what comes from the heart.

—MARTHA WASHINGTON

The right of conscience and private judgment is unalienable, and it is truly the interest of all mankind to unite themselves into one body for the liberty, free exercise, and unmolested enjoyment of this right.

—EZRA STILES

Cheerfulness in most cheerful people is the rich and satisfying result of strenuous discipline.

—EDWIN PERCY WHIPPLE

Our friends interpret the world and ourselves to us, if we take them tenderly and truly.

—AMOS BRONSON ALCOTT

The greatest crime is not developing your potential. When you do what you do best, you are helping not only yourself, but the world.

—ROGER WILLIAMS

A little flattery will support a man through great fatigue.

—JAMES MONROE

Happiness is the natural flower of duty.

—PHILLIPS BROOKS

The happiness of the domestic fireside is the first boon of mankind.

—THOMAS JEFFERSON

Something attempted, something done
Has earned a night's repose.

—HENRY WADSWORTH
LONGFELLOW

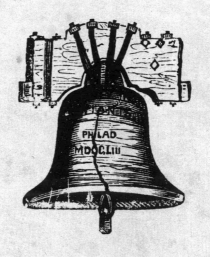

These Truths Shall Endure

Though the challenges faced by the early American thinkers and doers may have been unique to their time and place, the lessons they learned are timeless and universal. They experienced setbacks, overcame obstacles, embraced hope and rejected failure. In repeating these self-evident truths, we endeavor to repeat their success.

Facts are stubborn things; and whatever may be our wishes, our inclinations, or the dictates of our passion, they cannot alter the state of facts and evidence.

—JOHN ADAMS

Love carries through many difficulties easily and makes heavy burdens light.

—JOHN COTTON

Falsehood is cowardice, the truth courage.

—HOSEA BALLOU

Villainy wears many masks; none so dangerous as the mask of virtue.

—WASHINGTON IRVING

One great error is that we suppose mankind more honest than they are.

—ALEXANDER HAMILTON

All true ambition and aspiration are without comparisons.

—HENRY WARD BEECHER

In every human Breast, God has implanted a Principle, which we call Love of Freedom; it is impatient of Oppression, and pants for Deliverance.

—PHILLIS WHEATLEY

The greatest tyrannies are always perpetuated in the name of the noblest causes.

—THOMAS PAINE

Wit is an unexpected explosion of thought.

—EDWIN PERCY WHIPPLE

The best advice I can give…is to be strict in your discipline; that is, to require nothing unreasonable of your officers and men, but see that whatever is required be punctually complied with.

—GEORGE WASHINGTON

To believe all men honest is folly. To believe none is something worse.

—JOHN ADAMS

Exaggeration is a blood relation to falsehood and nearly as blamable.

—HOSEA BALLOU

Ambition is not a weakness unless it be disproportioned to the capacity.

—GEORGE S. HILLARD

The tongue is the only instrument that gets sharper with use.

—WASHINGTON IRVING

The truth is that all men having power ought to be mistrusted.

—JAMES MADISON

It is better to spread trust all around than to hand out money!

—JAMES MONROE

No man is prejudiced in favor of a thing knowing it to be wrong. He is attached to it on the belief of it being right.

—THOMAS PAINE

As we are, so we do; and as we do, so is it done to us; we are the builders of our fortunes.

—RALPH WALDO EMERSON

We too often bind ourselves by authorities rather than by the truth.

—LUCRETIA MOTT

The world is my country, all mankind are my brethren, and to do good is my religion.

—THOMAS PAINE

But truth is most likely to be exhibited by the general sense of contemporaries, when the feelings of the heart can be expressed without suffering itself to be disguised by the prejudices of man.

—MERCY OTIS WARREN

A pack of jackasses led by a lion is superior to a pack of lions led by a jackass.

—GEORGE WASHINGTON

Dignity is often a veil between us and the real truth of things.

—EDWIN PERCY WHIPPLE

No man for any considerable period can wear one face to himself and another to the multitude, without finally getting bewildered as to which may be the true.

—NATHANIEL HAWTHORNE

You know that women are always looked upon as nothing; but we are your mothers; you are our sons. Our cry is all for peace; let it continue. This peace must last forever. Let your women's sons be ours; let our sons be yours. Let your women hear our words.

—NANYEHI

Men often oppose a thing merely because they have had no agency in planning it, or because it may have been planned by those whom they dislike.

—ALEXANDER HAMILTON

It is easier to build strong children than to repair broken men.

—FREDERICK DOUGLASS

As men neither fear nor respect what has been made contemptible, all honor to him who makes oppression laughable as well as detestable.

—EDWIN PERCY WHIPPLE

This time, like all times, is a very good one, if we but know what to do with it.

—RALPH WALDO EMERSON

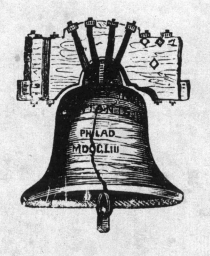

Conclusion

AMERICA HAS ALWAYS BEEN A NATION IN flux. The vision of our founding fathers and mothers saw the limits and possibilities in our country's growth—all while providing a language to understand the complexities of being good citizens of the United States.

They urged temperance and patience while insisting on an impassioned, vigorous pursuit of liberty. They advised as to the assiduous maintenance of good character while cautioning that the seeds of tyranny and self-promotion exist in all of us.

Early American leaders embraced contradiction because they understood the imperfection in human nature. Only in recognizing our limitations can we attempt to reach beyond them to create a more perfect union.

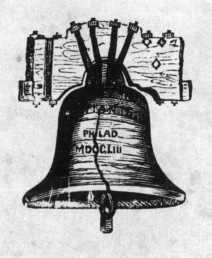

PHILAD
MDCCLIII